ANCIENT AND MEDIEVAL PEOPLE

The Scandinavian Vikings

Louise Park
and Timothy Love

Marshall Cavendish Benchmark

This edition first published in 2010 in the United States of America by Marshall Cavendish Benchmark.

Marshall Cavendish Benchmark
99 White Plains Road
Tarrytown, NY 10591
www.marshallcavendish.us

All Internet sites were available and accurate when sent to press.

First published in 2009 by
MACMILLAN EDUCATION AUSTRALIA PTY LTD
15–19 Claremont Street, South Yarra 3141

Visit our website at www.macmillan.com.au or go directly to www.macmillanlibrary.com.au

Associated companies and representatives throughout the world.

Copyright © Louise Park 2009

Library of Congress Cataloging-in-Publication Data

Park, Louise, 1961–
   The Scandinavian Vikings / by Louise Park and Timothy Love.
      p. cm. – (Ancient and medieval people)
   Includes index.
   ISBN 978-0-7614-4445-9
   1. Vikings–Juvenile literature. 2. Scandinavia–History–To
   1397–Juvenile literature. 3. Scandinavia–Social life and
   customs–Juvenile literature. I. Love, Timothy. II. Title.
   DL66.P37 2009
   948'.022–dc22

                          2008055778

Edited by Julia Carlomagno
Text and cover design by Cristina Neri, Canary Graphic Design
Page layout by Cristina Neri, Canary Graphic Design
Photo research by Legend Images
Illustrations by Colby Heppéll, Giovanni Caselli and Paul Konye

Printed in the United States

Acknowledgments
The author and the publisher are grateful to the following for permission to reproduce
copyright material:

Front cover photo: Viking hut and boat courtesy of Shutterstock; parchment © Selahattin BAYRAM/
iStockphoto

Photos courtesy of: Background photos throughout: old paper © peter zelei/iStockphoto; mosaic tiles
© Hedda Gjerpen/iStockphoto; Viking runes © Olga Brovina/iStockphoto; Viking ship silhouette
© A-Digit/iStockphoto; Coo-ee Historical Picture Library, **15**, **30**; Tom Lovell/National Geographic/
Getty Images, **28**; Giovanni Caselli's Universal Library Unlimited, **6**, **7**, **14**, **17**, **20**, **21** (top left, top right,
centre and bottom right), **26**, **27**; © Denise Kappa/iStockphoto, **24**; Photodisc, **22-3**; Photolibrary/The
Bridgeman Art Library, **11**; Photolibrary/Guiziou Franck, **21** (bottom left); Photolibrary/Ken Gillham,
29; Photolibrary/Mary Evans Picture Library, **13**; Photolibrary/North Wind Pictures, **25**; Shutterstock, **4**
(Viking hut and boat); © Andrew Barker/Shutterstock, **10**; © Paul B. Moore/Shutterstock, **9**; Wikimedia
Commons, image by Bogdan Giusça, **12**.

Sources for quotes used in text: Quote from former US President George W. Bush, 2002, **25**.

While every care has been taken to trace and acknowledge copyright, the publisher tenders
their apologies for any accidental infringement where copyright has proved untraceable.
Where the attempt has been unsuccessful, the publisher welcomes information that would redress
the situation.

The authors and publisher wish to advise that to the best of their ability they have tried to verify
dates, facts, and the spelling of personal names and terminology. The accuracy and reliability of some
information on ancient civilizations is difficult in instances where detailed records were not kept or did
not survive.

Contents

Glossary Words

When a word is printed in **bold**, you can look up its meaning in the Glossary on page 31.

Who Were the Scandinavian Vikings?

The Scandinavian Vikings were people from the Scandinavian countries of Denmark, Sweden, and Norway. They were also known as the Norse people. In the late 700s CE these **warriors** left their homes and sailed all over northern Europe in **longships**.

Viking Settlements

Viking settlements existed in Europe and North America. In the 700s, Vikings began sailing and exploring new lands. Between 800 and 1066, Vikings conquered and colonized areas in England, Scotland, Ireland, and western and central Europe. Some Vikings founded settlements in Iceland while others explored North America, including Greenland. The largest Viking settlement was in York, England.

Scandinavian Vikings Timeline

850
Vikings capture the city of York in England

900
Vikings launch raids along the Mediterranean coast

911
Viking chief Rollo founds the Viking kingdom of Normandy in France

850

900

950

866
A Viking kingdom is established in York

981
Viking explorer Erik the Red discovers the island of Greenland

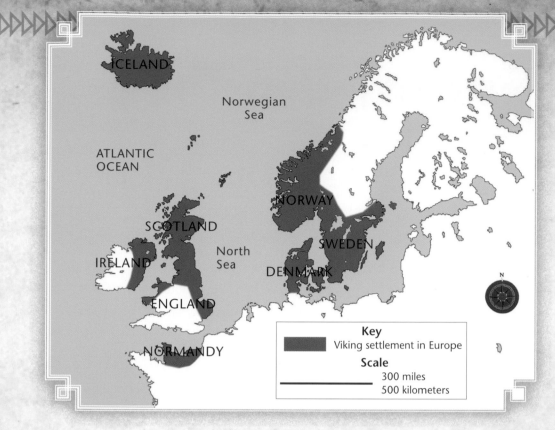

The Scandinavian Vikings founded settlements in northern Europe.

When Did the Scandinavian Vikings Exist?

The Scandinavian Vikings were most powerful between 789 and 1066. Most Vikings were explorers, **traders**, farmers, **craftspeople**, and boat builders. They traveled to new lands in search of better farmland and living conditions, or new trading partners. Other Vikings invaded lands and **pillaged** them. They were known as **raiders** and sea pirates.

By the late 1000s, Vikings found that they could no longer defeat the armies they were fighting against. Many Vikings had also converted to Christianity, and had settled in different places. In 1066, the Battle of Hastings took place and the decline of the Scandinavian Vikings began.

WHAT'S IN A NAME?

Viking

The name *Viking* comes from the Old Norse word *vikingr*. It most likely means "one who comes from the **inlet**." By the end of the Viking period, the name was given to all those who traveled across oceans to pillage lands.

1000
Viking explorer Leif Eriksson explores the coast of North America

1016–1035
King Canute rules England

1066
The Battle of Hastings marks the decline of the Scandinavian Vikings

1000   1050   1100

Viking Social Classes

In Viking society, people were divided into social classes. Within each social class there were different types of Vikings who each performed different roles.

The Slaves

Viking slaves were known as thralls and they were the lowest social class in Viking society. Thralls had to work for a master, who had the power to decide whether they lived or died. It was not uncommon for a master to offer his thrall as a human sacrifice during the funeral of a senior Viking. Thralls could also earn their freedom through hard work and dedication to their masters.

Quick Facts

How Did People Become Thralls?

People became thralls by birth or circumstance.

❖ Most people became thralls by being born into thrall families.

❖ People taken prisoner by Vikings also became thralls.

Boys from thrall families had to work for masters from a young age.

The Free People

The free people did not work for masters. Every free man had to train to fight as a warrior. There were several types of free people.

❖ Bondsmen were thralls who had been set free.

❖ Farmers, fishermen, traders, and builders built and traded goods and produced food.

❖ Leidings were **tenants** who rented or leased farmland. Often a tenant would give part of his **produce** to the landowner as rent.

❖ Freeholders owned farmland and had to show that the land had been owned by their family for at least six **generations**.

The Aristocracy

The aristocracy was the most powerful social class in Viking society. It was made up of the chieftains, earls, and kings. Chieftains and earls were wealthy landowners and important leaders within their villages. Kings ruled over Viking settlements known as kingdoms.

Viking boat builders built longships for warriors to sail in.

SPOTLIGHT ON Longships

Vikings were skilled sailors and boat builders. They built all kinds of boats that were used for different purposes. Their most famous type of boats were longships, or *drekkar*.

— Spotlight On —

WHAT: Longships

ALSO KNOWN AS: Drekkar

USED BY: Viking raiders

What Were Longships?

Longships carried large numbers of warriors on Viking raids. They were usually owned by members of the aristocracy because they were very expensive to build.

BOW AND STERN
A longship had a tapered **bow** and **stern**, which allowed Vikings to sail forward and backward without having to turn the ship around. This meant they could escape quickly.

SAILS
Woolen sails were attached to the mast. Many sails were dyed red, which signaled danger and made enemies fearful.

CREW
An average longship had twenty-five rowers to work the oars. It also had shields to protect the crew from spears and arrows during battle.

WOOD AND ANIMAL FUR
Longships were built from pine or oak to keep them light. Spaces between planks were blocked with tarred animal fur to keep the boat watertight.

DRAFT
The body had a low **draft**, which allowed longships to sail in shallow waters.

Longship Crews

Most longships required between twenty and thirty men to row the oars when the wind stopped and the sails could not be used. A **helmsman** steered while a lookout watched for dangerous rocks or land. The rest of the space on the boat was filled with Viking warriors, weapons, food, and drink.

Vikings often took several longships, each filled with soldiers, on raids.

What You Should Know About...

Longships

❖ Longships were important symbols to Vikings. They were used at the burials of great Viking warriors, to send them into the **afterlife**.

❖ The largest longship ever found was 230 feet (70 meters) long. It could easily hold up to four hundred Viking warriors. Scientific tests on the timber suggest that it was built around 1025.

❖ Vikings created the world's first sleeping bags in order to sleep comfortably on longships.

Viking Raids

Vikings did not have a professional army or complex battle tactics. They were most successful when conducting raids and surprise attacks.

Raids

Raids were often launched on places close to shorelines because they could be attacked quickly. These places were raided to find:

❖ money and treasure

❖ new land to settle

❖ new trading partners

During raids, Vikings took weapons, money, precious metals, jewelry, clothing, and people who could be sold as slaves. A small raid might only involve enough warriors to fill 2 longships, while a large raid might include more than 350 longships filled with warriors.

Surprise Attacks

Surprise attacks began during the late 790s. Vikings would plan these attacks in winter and carry them out in summer. They often took place early in the morning. Viking warriors sailed in quickly and robbed the villages of anything valuable they could find. They set buildings on fire and left as quickly as they came.

The first recorded Viking raid occurred on the island of Lindisfarne.

The First Viking Raid

The first recorded Viking raid took place in 793 at a monastery on the island of Lindisfarne, off the northeastern coast of Scotland. Monasteries were a prime target for Vikings in the early years of raiding because it was believed that they held great wealth within their walls. The monks at Lindisfarne recorded the raid in books. They described these Vikings as bloodthirsty **barbarians**.

Quick Facts

Did Vikings Have a Reputation for Being Fierce?

Vikings had a reputation for being fierce in almost every country they raided.

❖ Viking raids were so successful that the government of Paris paid Vikings not to attack. They were given part of France, known as Normandy, to **appease** them.

❖ **Berserkers** were warriors who went into a crazy, fearless state during battle. In this state they felt no pain and believed they were bears. They displayed almost superhuman strength.

❖ When Viking warriors were outnumbered, they fought hand-to-hand combat. They would form a tight circle and fight to the death.

Vikings would often take villagers by surprise by sailing into a village just as the Sun was rising.

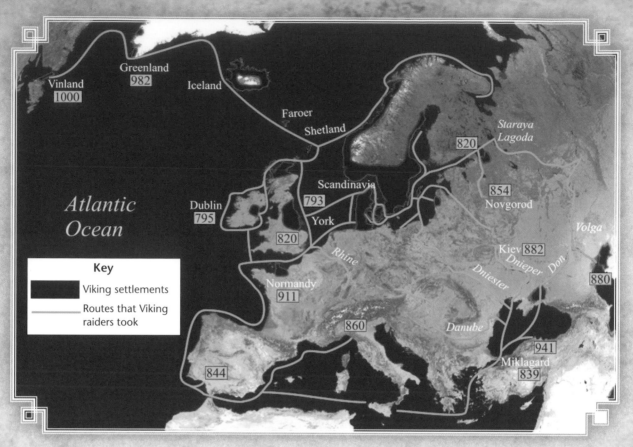

This map shows the routes that Viking raiders took to raid countries in Europe between 793 and 1000, and their settlements.

Phases of Viking Raids

Historians have classified Viking raids into three distinct periods.

❖ The first phase covered the period 790–840.

❖ The second phase is believed to cover the period 841–875.

❖ The final phase covered the period 876–911.

The First Phase (790–840)

During the first phase of Viking raids, small groups of Viking warriors landed and conducted quick surprise attacks before retreating. These raids were conducted mainly along the coasts of England and France. One of the sites attacked most often during this phase of raids was the monastery of Lindisfarne. Vikings first attacked this monastery in 793 and the raids continued into the next century. The monks could not defend themselves against these attacks and eventually fled the island in 875.

The Second Phase (841–875)

The second phase was marked by larger Viking raids. During this period, a village could be raided by up to 350 Viking longships. Vikings began traveling across the Mediterranean Sea and attacking places as far away as northern Africa. For the first time ever, Viking warriors began to build settlements on foreign soil. This extended the Viking empire and made people in unconquered areas begin to view Viking warriors as a threat.

The Third Phase (876–911)

During this final phase of raids, Viking warriors continued to raid areas along both sides of the English Channel. Vikings formed permanent settlements in Ireland, Iceland, and Russia.

As Viking raids grew in size, hundreds of longships and thousands of warriors would land off the coasts of countries.

IN PROFILE: King Canute

Canute was the son of King Sweyn, a Danish king. He was a Viking warrior who went on to become the first Viking king of England. Between 1016 and 1035, he ruled over England and some of the Scandinavian countries, including Denmark and Norway.

King Canute is remembered as the first king to rule successfully over a united England. He brought peace to England because he also ruled the Viking lands and could stop Vikings from conducting raids on England. During his reign, trade and Christianity **flourished**. He was seen as a fair and decent king.

Notable Moment

In 1013, Canute helped his father conquer England. Sweyn became king, but he died a year later. Ethelred II, the king who had fled during Sweyn's attack, was made king once more. In 1015, Canute led an attack on England to **reclaim** the throne. Canute fought many battles against Ethelred II and after he died, against his son, Edmund.

Defeating King Edmund

After many battles, Canute finally defeated King Edmund in Ashingdon in 1016. A **treaty** was signed that allowed Edmund to rule over southern England while Canute ruled over the rest of England. When Edmund died, Canute became the king of all of England.

King Canute Timeline

1010	1015	1020

1013
Invades England with his father, Sweyn

1015
Returns to England to fight Ethelred and takes control of most of England

1016
Defeats King Edmund and becomes king of England

After his defeat, King Edmund (left) agreed to give Canute control of most of England.

Expanding the Empire

Over the next twelve years, King Canute expanded his empire. In 1019, he took control of Denmark after the death of his brother, King Harald. In 1026, Canute took control of Scandinavia during a battle known as Holy River. In 1028, Canute sailed to Norway. The Norwegians were unable to put up a fight and Canute took control of Norway, too.

What You Should Know About...

King Canute

❖ He once gave a mansion as a gift to William Peuse, an Englishman who warned him of a planned ambush. He also gave Peuse a horn bearing the words "ynge Knoul gave Wyllyam Peuse thys horne to holde by thy lande."

❖ Today, this horn is kept in the Victoria and Albert Museum in London, England.

1025   **1030**   **1035**

1019
Claims the throne of Denmark after his brother's death

1026
Takes control of Scandinavia

1028
Becomes king of Norway

Viking Homes

Most Vikings lived in longhouses on farms or in towns.

Longhouses

Viking families lived together in wood or stone buildings called longhouses. Longhouses were similar to big halls, and they were up to 98 ft (30 m) long. Each longhouse was home to children, parents, grandparents, and anyone else who was a member of the owner's **extended family**. If the family owned thralls, they lived in the longhouse too.

The walls of a longhouse were wooden and the roof was **thatched**. Along the walls were benches for sitting and sleeping. Animals were kept in a stable at the end of the hall. A fire heated the longhouse and was used for cooking. Families used lamps that burned wax or blubber.

Thatched roof

Windows for smoke to escape

Wooden walls

Stable for animals

Fire for cooking and heating

Benches for sitting and sleeping

This cross section shows the features of a typical Viking longhouse.

Women in Viking homes cooked, made clothes, and looked after young children.

Farms and Towns

Many Viking families worked on farms. Animals such as cows, goats, pigs, and sheep were kept on the farm. Viking traders, craftspeople, and blacksmiths often lived in towns, where there was more opportunity to sell goods and offer services. Traders and craftspeople sold and traded clothing, jewelry, cups and bowls, cloth, animals, and food. Blacksmiths shaped metal into tools and weapons.

Quick Facts

What Roles Did Women Play in Viking Homes?

Viking women played many important roles, including running the longhouse, healing sick people, and looking after children.

❖ Women milked cows, made butter and cheese, and preserved meats. They ran the farms while the men were away.

❖ Women made clothing and cloth blankets, and treated sick family members with herbs. They also looked after their children, who did not go to school but learned from the family at home.

❖ Viking women had more rights than women in many other societies of the time. They could **inherit** and own land, divorce, remarry, and become traders.

Clothing and Jewelry

The types of clothing and jewelry worn by Vikings depended on how wealthy they were. Jewelry was worn as a sign of wealth as well as for decoration.

Viking Clothing

Viking clothing was designed to suit the work Vikings did and the environment they were in. Most Viking clothing was made from wool and dyed different colors using dyes made from vegetables, berries, and soil.

A Viking man wore:

❖ long, fitted woolen trousers

❖ linen or wool shirts

❖ a tunic

❖ a leather belt

❖ a woolen cloak

❖ leather shoes

A Viking woman wore:

❖ an ankle-length linen dress

❖ an apron or pinafore, secured at the shoulders with brooches

❖ a leather belt

❖ a shawl fastened with a brooch near the neck

❖ leather shoes

Earls and kings often wore imported silk shirts and furs. Wealthy women wore silk smocks. Married women wore headscarves that knotted underneath each ear and covered the top of their head.

Viking women often hung household tools, such as scissors and knives, from the brooches at their shoulders while men often wore woolen cloaks.

Viking Jewelry

Vikings wore jewelry for decoration and to display their wealth. The wealthier and more important Vikings were, the more jewelry they wore. Viking jewelry was mostly made from silver, bronze, gold, and bone. The designs of early Viking jewelry were based on everyday elements and patterns found in their local surroundings. However, after Vikings began to raids other countries, the designs of Viking jewelry began to show the influences of these countries.

Types of Jewelry

Viking jewelers made many types of jewelry, including:

❖ brooches

❖ clasps

❖ finger rings

❖ arm bands

❖ bracelets

❖ pendants and necklaces

Wealthy Viking men wore many types of jewelry to display their wealth and importance.

Armor and Weapons

All free men were trained to fight and were expected to go into battle. Most wore little armor, and carried their everyday tools into battle.

Viking Armor and Helmets

Few Vikings wore armor, although most wore helmets. Most warriors were farmers and craftsmen, and they wore their everyday clothing into battle. Wealthy Vikings wore chain mail coats over their clothes. Helmets were made from leather or metal. Some included a strip of metal along the center to make them stronger. This metal often extended down to give protection to the eyes and nose. Viking helmets did not have horns, as they often do in books and films.

In battle, wealthy Vikings wore chain mail coats, and most Vikings wore metal helmets that came down over their noses.

Viking Weapons

Viking men used their everyday tools, such as axes and knives, as weapons. They also used shields, swords, and spears.

A Viking warrior's most treasured possession was his sword. Most Viking swords were double-edged and had a decorated hilt. The blade was carved with runes for good luck and the tip was kept pointed and sharp.

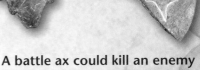

A battle ax could kill an enemy with one swift blow. It was used in close-range combat.

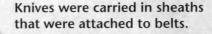

Spears were thrown at enemies. Each spear had a sharp metal tip shaped like a leaf. Many Viking spears were decorated with runes.

Knives were carried in sheaths that were attached to belts.

Viking shields were round and wooden. A metal boss, or handguard, protected the owner's hand. Some warriors painted patterns on their shields.

WHAT'S IN A NAME?

Runes

The letters in the ancient Viking alphabet were called runes. Runes were carved into wood or stone. The letters were all made of straight lines so that they were easy to carve.

Viking Expansion

As Viking populations grew, the need for new farmland increased. Groups of Viking warriors explored new territories to colonize.

Viking Explorers

Viking explorers colonized parts of England, Scotland, Ireland, and western Europe, and discovered Greenland and North America. Their voyages led to permanent settlements in Iceland, where no humans had previously lived.

1 793
The first Viking raids on Ireland. About sixty years later the Viking settlement of Dublin was started

2 839–840
The first Viking attacks and settlement in Russia and the Ukraine

3 845
Invasion and exploration of Spain and Germany

4 860
Viking exploration of northern Africa

5 860
Viking exploration of the western Italian coast

6 860
Vikings are believed to have discovered Iceland

Contribution to Exploration and Discovery

While Viking warriors are well known for conducting raids, they are less known for their contribution to exploration and discovery. One of the main reasons for this is that Vikings did not record the locations of their discoveries or the details of their voyages. The colonies they established in North America, including Greenland, did not survive. These lands were re-discovered by Spanish and English explorers in the 1400s and 1500s, approximately five hundred years after the Vikings.

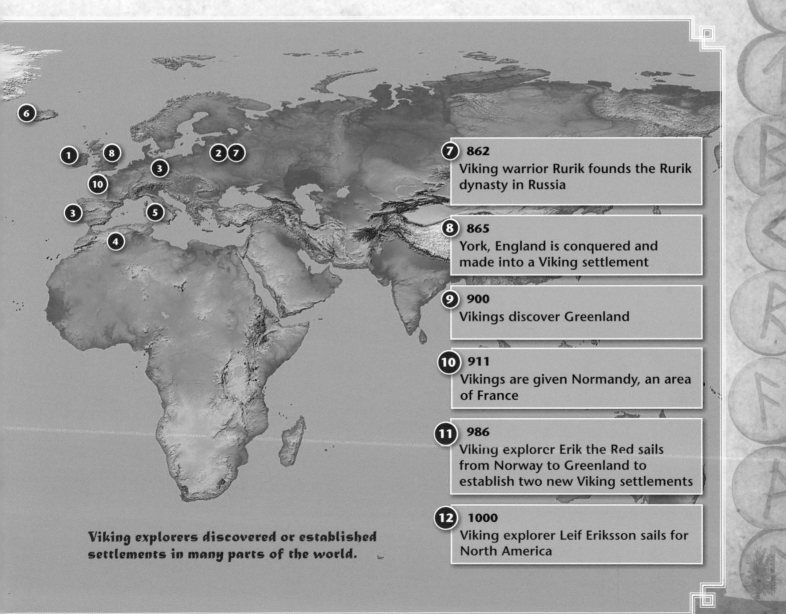

Viking explorers discovered or established settlements in many parts of the world.

7 862
Viking warrior Rurik founds the Rurik dynasty in Russia

8 865
York, England is conquered and made into a Viking settlement

9 900
Vikings discover Greenland

10 911
Vikings are given Normandy, an area of France

11 986
Viking explorer Erik the Red sails from Norway to Greenland to establish two new Viking settlements

12 1000
Viking explorer Leif Eriksson sails for North America

IN PROFILE: Leif Eriksson

Leif Eriksson was the son of Viking explorer Erik the Red. Leif, who was born in Iceland, is remembered as a great explorer who led many expeditions.

Eriksson explored many parts of North America during his voyages. He earned the name "Leif the Lucky" because he rarely encounted trouble on his voyages, which brought great wealth to the Viking countries. He also discovered lands that were good for new Viking settlements.

Notable Moment

In 1000, Eriksson sailed in search of new lands. He landed in a place he named Vinland and built a small settlement there. Today, this place is known as Newfoundland. It is located in the Canadian province of Newfoundland and Labrador.

Leif Eriksson Timeline

960
970
980

960
Born in Iceland to the Viking explorer Erik the Red

980
Travels with his father to colonize Greenland

Leif Eriksson and his men anchored their longship off the coast of North America and rowed ashore.

Leif Eriksson Day

The United States celebrates Leif Eriksson Day on October 9 each year to honor the first European to set foot on North American soil.

*More than one thousand years ago, Leif Eriksson and his crew journeyed across the Atlantic seeking unknown lands. Their pioneering spirit of courage, determination, and discovery helped to open the world to new exploration.... Each October, we join our friends in Iceland, Norway, Denmark, Sweden, and Finland in honoring this historic voyage and in celebrating the strong **transatlantic** bonds that exist between those countries and the United States.*

FORMER U.S. PRESIDENT GEORGE W. BUSH, 2002

What You Should Know About...

Leif Eriksson

❖ Leif Eriksson became the leader of the Norse colony in Greenland. He also explored the western part of Greenland.

❖ During his visit to Norway, Eriksson converted to Christianity. Many Vikings would join him in converting to Christianity over the following years.

990   1000   1010

984
Sails to Norway to take gifts to the king

1000
Discovers Baffin Island and Vinland

1001
Returns to Greenland

Religion and Mythology

Vikings were originally **pagan**, and they worshiped many gods.

Asgard

Vikings believed the gods lived above them in a world called Asgard. Asgard was accessed via a rainbow bridge. All Vikings believed that if they led good lives and worshiped the gods they would live in Asgard once they died. Men and women were buried with the belongings they would need in Asgard.

Vikings believed that Asgard was divided into approximately twelve realms and each god lived in a different realm. The most important realm was Valhalla, where the king of the gods, Odin, lived. Norse gods supposedly ate apples of youth to keep them young forever.

Most Viking warriors wanted to go to the realm of Valhalla when they died.

Worshiping Gods

In the early Viking period, Vikings worshiped the gods outdoors. Ceremonies often took place within circles of stones or under trees. In later years, Vikings built temples in which to worship the gods. Animals and even humans were sacrificed to the gods in these temples.

Viking Gods

There were six important Viking gods.

❖ Odin was the king of the gods. He was the god of war, wisdom, and poetry. Brave warriors went to his palace in Valhalla when they died. The legend of Odin says that he gave an eye in exchange for wisdom.

❖ Freya was married to Odin. She was the goddess of love, beauty, and destiny. She had the right to claim half of the bravest warriors' souls when they died.

❖ Frey was Freya's brother. He was the god of nature. Vikings made sacrifices to Frey to ensure that their crops would grow well.

❖ Thor was the son of Odin. He was the god of thunder, which was associated with strength.

❖ Loki was half-god and half-giant. He represented evil and cunning.

❖ Hel was the daughter of Loki. She ruled over Niflhem, the icy land of the dead.

Thor carried a magic hammer to defend himself from enemies.

Viking Burials and Funerals

It was important for Vikings to send their dead into the afterlife correctly. Vikings believed that if the dead were buried in a manner that reflected their social status on Earth, they would enter Asgard with the same social status.

Longship Burials

Vikings believed that funerals had to be handled properly to ensure that the dead were at peace in the afterlife. Great warriors and members of the aristocracy were often set to rest in their longships. Sometimes these longships were buried and sometimes they were set on fire and sent out to sea. Vikings were buried with the belongings they may need in the afterlife, such as weapons or even animals. Sometimes a thrall was also sacrificed at the burial. The thrall was thought to travel with the master into the afterlife to serve him there. Offerings were also placed into longships or at burial sites. Different offerings were given to people according to their social status.

In a traditional Viking warrior burial, a longship containing the dead and their belongings was set on fire and sent out to sea.

The Oseberg Longship

One of the wealthiest Viking longships ever discovered was the Oseberg longship. Archaeologists believe it was built between 815 and 820. The longboat was thought to hold the body of a queen and her thrall, and was filled with items for the afterlife. Belongings found in the longship included beds, an ornate cart, wooden chests, riding equipment, sledges, and twelve horses. The longship was buried under layers of peat and stones when it was found by a Norwegian farmer. It was **excavated** in 1904.

Burials Without a Longship

Not all Vikings received an expensive longship burial. Some warriors were **cremated** inside stone ships, or stones that had been laid on the ground in the shape of ship. Other warriors were burned on a pyre, which was a bundle of sticks that was set on fire. Women were often buried in wagons or carts, and thralls were often simply buried in a hole without a gravestone.

Viking burial sites, such as this one, can still be found in many of the European countries colonized by Vikings.

The Decline of the Scandinavian Vikings

The power of the Scandinavian Vikings began to decline following the Battle of Hastings in 1066. After this time, many Vikings converted to Christianity and stopped raiding other countries.

The Battle of Hastings

Most historians mark the decline of the Scandinavian Vikings with the Battle of Hastings. In this battle William, Duke of Normandy, conquered England by overthrowing the Viking king, Harold II. Over time, Christianity became the official religion in many countries and many Vikings became Christians. Vikings began to settle in Scandinavia, rather than exploring and raiding other countries. By the 1200s, the Viking way of life had ceased to exist.

Legacies of the Scandinavian Vikings

Vikings left many legacies, or reminders, of their existence.

❖ Many English words have Viking origins. The word *Thursday* comes from the Viking "Thor's Day." The words *egg*, *husband,* and *law* also have Viking origins.

❖ Museums house many Viking objects, including longboats, tools, and clothing.

❖ Many Europeans today are of Viking **descent**.

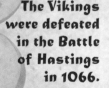

The Vikings were defeated in the Battle of Hastings in 1066.

Glossary

afterlife   The soul's life after death.

appease   Satisfy.

barbarians   People who are considered to be cruel, violent, and uncivilized.

berserkers   Viking warriors who fought fiercely in battles.

bow   The front end of a ship.

chain mail   A type of flexible armor made from joined metal links or scales.

colonized   Created settlements of people, or colonies.

conquered   Took control or defeated by using force.

converted   Changed to.

craftspeople   Skilled people who made armor and weapons.

cremated   Burned to ashes after death.

cunning   Clever and cruel.

descent   Part of a line of family history or ancestors.

draft   The depth of a boat, measured from the deepest point to the waterline.

excavated   Dug up.

extended family   The relatives of a person, including grandparents, aunts, uncles, and cousins.

flourished   Grown in strength or increased.

generation   Group of people living at the same time.

helmsman   The man who steers a longship.

inherit   Receive something from a relative, often after they have died.

inlet   An opening, such as a bay or a cove, along a coast.

longships   Viking ships used to carry large numbers of warriors on raids.

navigate   Direct a voyage.

offerings   Gifts that could be used in the afterlife, such as weapons.

pagan   People who did not follow one god.

pillaged   Stole valuable goods.

produce   Food grown through farming.

raiders   People who try to take over other countries.

realms   Areas or regions.

reclaim   Take back.

runes   Letters in the Viking alphabet.

sacrifice   An offering given to please the gods.

social status   The position of a person within a group of people

stern   The back end of a ship.

tenants   People who live on land owned by another.

thatched   Covered with a material such as straw or leaves.

traders   People who buy and sell items.

transatlantic   Spanning across the Atlantic Ocean.

treaty   A written agreement between two states or countries.

warriors   Soldiers with great skill in battle.

Index